forget
·sadness·
grass

forget ·sadness· grass

百合

POEMS BY
ANTONY DI NARDO

RONSDALE

RONSDALE PRESS
3350 West 21st Avenue
Vancouver, B.C., Canada V6S 1G7
www.ronsdalepress.com

Typesetting: Julie Cochrane, in New Baskerville 11 pt on 13.5
Cover Design: Julie Cochrane
Paper: Lynx Opaque Ultra 60 lb.

Ronsdale Press wishes to thank the following for their support of its publishing program: the Canada Council for the Arts, the Government of Canada, the British Columbia Arts Council, and the Province of British Columbia through the Book Publishing Tax Credit Program.

Library and Archives Canada Cataloguing in Publication

Title: Forget, sadness, grass / poems by Antony Di Nardo.
Names: Di Nardo, Antony, 1949– author.
Description: "Bai he" (transliterated from the Chinese).
Identifiers: Canadiana (print) 20220279136 | Canadiana (ebook) 20220279772 | ISBN 9781553806684 (softcover) | ISBN 9781553806691 (HTML) | ISBN 9781553806707 (PDF)
Classification: LCC PS8607.I535 F67 2022 | DDC C811/.6—dc23

At Ronsdale Press we are committed to protecting the environment. To this end we are working with Canopy and printers to phase out our use of paper produced from ancient forests. This book is one step towards that goal.

Printed in Canada by Rapido Livres Books, Montreal, QC

for Annie,
la meliora hortulanus

"That was my Lo," she said, "and these are my lilies."
"Yes," I said, "yes. They are beautiful, beautiful, beautiful."

—VLADIMIR NABOKOV, *Lolita*

" . . . she always had the feeling that it was very,
very dangerous to live even one day."

—VIRGINIA WOOLF, *Mrs. Dalloway*

"I once believed a single line
in a Chinese poem could change
forever how blossoms fell"

—LEONARD COHEN, *For E.J.P.*

CONTENTS

– II –
"Wild Thing"

Forget-Sadness-Grass

Forget-Sadness-Grass, written as 百合 in ancient Chinese characters, is one of the many names given to the common daylily by the ancient poets of the T'ang Dynasty who often travelled far from home and longed to return to those they left behind.

Memories of home, a surge of nostalgia for the comfort of family and friends, the eyes of a lover remembered, these poets wrote longingly about the day they'd return, collecting along the way impressions of the countryside, seeds for an idea they'd germinate on bits of dry and matted parchment stuffed in shoulder bags.

The road is often inspiring to a poet and verses make the journey not quite as arduous.

Upon returning home, after warm embraces, it was customary to offer their loved one a flower (the bright bloom of the lily was most highly prized), as well as a *shih*, a poem composed along the way to be recited after the sun had gone down.

On their travels, it was the tall, grass-like leaves of the daylilies that waved to them from the fields, like the lover who would soon greet them and, inspired by the promise of a blossom that soon would appear, the sadness felt at the thought of being far from home was forgotten.

~ I ~

Daylily

百合

An escape of Asiatic origin

the lily turns 360 and circumscribes the globe

grown tall enough to be the sky

unwavering even unto wind or weather, said Li Bai

with a roof above its head and roots beneath
        the clouds
     for when the sun descends
          and the lily's left behind

Daylily

Tawny-touched, orange crushed,
              the plain insides of a pumpkin
        thrust into receiving hands

Faded cheeks, a lily's face redoubled in the pond,
        the colour of koi
                too slippery to snatch
                      from the surface of the sun

Exhausted when the moon comes out

Exuberance in all there is to know
        when daylight turns its head and looks

Shih

Profusion,
       abundance,
the uninterrupted gaze of sunlight
           from dawn to when
the eyes shut tight

Sun-tall and slight, they swing and
                       sway
under the bright lights
         of August and July

A nudge from the first hint of morning
       sufficient to open their eyes

They're magnificent, pondside, a stint
     as beauty
         in numbers
              synchronized
     like bluebells and cockle shells
               all in row

I Tell Them Lies

I tell them lies—
That I'm an action figure
               born of an Easter egg

That I've been Stan Lee for most my life

I tell them my invisibility cloak is solid-state
          made of longing, pixels, words like these

I talk to them in my sleep and keep them company

I ruffle feathers
         the evening leaves are falling from my head

I blend in, the lilies know my face

But like Li Bai I'm never home
           which is why I have so much to say

Like Lovers

Li Bai knew a thing or two about lilies—
          he'd write about their tongues,
                              their lips,
the cusp of moon between their leaves

A lily in his hands would ooze a rapture,
shed painted petals, inspire perfected tropes—
stamens,
          pistils, the stammering of bees,
every stem an idiom spoken of
                    as *Hemerocallis Fulva*

Like lovers perform duets, perfume their triolets,
he'd slip a verse between the sheets,
          pluck shadows from the late-night moon
and recite by heart odes yet unwritten to
                    the lily and the vulva

His pen raised
          and poised,
                    eager at the garden gate

Dialectical Lily

First light, I raise my head
                      and set myself on my own
                                          two feet

I walk the length of the hall to the kitchen
out the door
down the steps
past the front gate
and into the world of no turning back

First light, first thought, a lily takes a single step
                   the only one there is to take
             and then returns
                              to where it started

Migrant Bloom

The orange daylily forms dense stands that
exclude native vegetation, and is often
mistaken for a native species.
                                    —Wikipedia

December is far from July
        the *Lilium* far
        from the truth of the asphodel

And the daylily, like me, a settler, a migrant
        to the banks of the pond

Far from its sources

Far from its origins

Far from midday and the terrible
                        truth of December

Lullaby

Restless as a mountain torrent,
                 sometimes a young city,
sometimes stirred
      by the snap of a broken branch

but not a word from the lily,
not until the sun declines and the moon peers
      into the eyes of the turgid pond

It's at that time she leans her head
              towards mine
and sings herself to sleep,
      sinks to the bottom of the bed

Motherhood

Lilies never needed an actual womb
        to be born, an actual shell to explode
into petals, a name to be called in for supper,
        a pair of jeans, rattles or bibs

The lily never needed to know the difference
        between one place or another,
where one sat and what one stood for

It never needed to be held down
        or be kept home

Never needed to shape a heart
        with both hands
            on my chest

And for the clouds to turn colour
And the clouds to keep moving

A Lily's Flight

You need your head to nod all day
above a tuft of morning grass,
                    your arms outstretched,
your cheeks like petals upward facing
        on a steady stem

The work of daylight
        opens wide and cups the sun entirely

A robin's flight disturbs the airwaves,
        the robin with his tail erect,
                    his wings intact,
                            his beak shut tight

By six the sun will have gone the other way, far
                from where you got your start—
then you'll take your wings
            and reach into the end of time

Shadows of a Late Afternoon

Shadows of a late afternoon
      lay down their heads
           and rest at the feet of the lilies

Across the great lawn,
         the greatest show on earth

I-beams of light raised high above the pillars
        to build a crystal palace

And without the sun
      there'd be no shadows, no shadows
for the lilies to see themselves as they are

Ditch Lily

A singular lily
          and six feet away

Of all the lilies,
     a fleeting blossom
          that captures the imagination
              of an entire forest

No thought of projecting itself out there
          further into the open plains,
             into fields of gold,
happy with the ditch it's in,
     taking up
          its sun-given space
             and nothing else

Journal Entry

Unrelenting sunlight, silence
(the silence of ornamentals, knots
on parcels no one can unravel
            without disturbing the peace),
and first thing this morning
            the lilies on their feet

Elsewhere, docks and decking everywhere
I looked
            sailing into landscape

The lilies dazed as usual
            by their own naturalizing beauty

When the sun had left
I found this poem by Tseng Jui
in a book from another century—

Flowers bloom and flowers fall, everyone knows;
Flowers
pretty as ever,
Men
vainly cursing old age.

Metaphysics

Metaphysics turns stones into blossoms,
     clouds into feathers spun
                    until they too rise and lift
the souls of fallen trees

Metaphysics has the power of daily decision,
     of putting words in your mouth,
               of changing
your mind from the dead of night
                    to waking day—
wings where once there were no wings

and lilies, eyes shut tight,
                    the heart close-fisted,
     waiting for the sun
to resurrect and break them open

And then what?

For a While

I would like to trade places with a daylily for a while
        the great lust of leaves
                        head in the affirmative
clouds within reach without ever leaving home

I would like to be a sure-fire thing
        a given, an understanding between
                        daybreak and sunset
an act of embellishment

I would like to stay put for a while, yet bendable
        touchable, easily seen
                        a crease in the fabric
a state of being just here for a while

Everything the Lily Knows

it knows for a day
the sound of rain, the sensation of molecules
             rubbing up against the skin
insects and the science of spreading your seeds

when the lily glows, it glows for that moment only
it throws itself into the act and struts its stuff
             across the stage
displays everything it knows, all it has, for just a day

the lily never sleeps: there is no in-between
one day and the next: there is no next
only life and death
             one moment on fire and then you're not

I Read Somewhere

I read somewhere
      that lilies come into the world to offer us respite
          from the mundane

and that we should never expect them to grow
      on stalks of clover
          or the rings of Saturn

and that truth is fragile, spurious in the act of telling,
      but like the lily short-lived yet everlasting
          if you keep it to yourself

Under Construction

Not every lily is a poem
                or comes with a poem

Not every lily has a poem in its pocket

Or looks like a poem when a poem is fresh and new

Or needs one to get through the day
                        or feel completed

Or finds one when it's not even looking for a poem

Or leaves one behind after it's gone
                    from the face of the earth

"We Are the Champions"

Almost the last of July
and summer's in full tilt
gathering up its skirts,
running off into the meadows

What better way
to spend a day in the country
where the radio plays a little
Freddie Mercury
and the lilies sway, sway,
and sing along

Accidental Heaven

I fool my heart because I love someone
The rock 'n' roll of my youth is sealed within
I can't sing but I sure know how to feed the songbirds
Studio sessions, early morning, early dusk
No one has the blues
Yet we're all singing
The Bose, the Pleiades, finches in the trees
My own pencil scratched across the score of lilies on the page

Deep Space

Mission accomplished

Satellites of the sun

The stillness of space in the morning

Sweet William's dead
Susan's on her way out
Daffodil's gone
Iris and Daisy are off to the side

And when Lily opens her eyes—
         deep space and nothing else

The Poet Said

One only writes in order to erase again

I stop mid-sentence
                    to collect my thoughts

What more to say about the sun?

Fiery petals open wide

The lily guides my hand across the page

I look from where I came

Thousands of Lilies

Lost among the flowers,
I wear my hat upside down
—Li Bai

Like Li Bai himself I wear my hat upside down
I make mistakes
I ridicule both left and right
I make you laugh
I've made you run on tears before

I feed the birds, my pockets full
I sleep and conjure rising suns

I count each day as first and last
There are 36,000 of them
                to a hundred years, says Li Bai
I believe he's right

And each day one must drain the cups
Walk out the door, put on a hat

Thousands of lilies in a single day
Ten thousand hats to make a sky

daylily

daylily   daylily   daylily   daylily   daylily   daylily
    daylily   daylily   daylily   daylily   daylily
daylily   daylily   daylily   daylily   daylily   daylily
    daylily   daylily   daylily   daylily   daylily
daylily   daylily   daylily   daylily   daylily   daylily
    daylily   daylily   daylily   daylily   daylily
daylily   daylily   daylily   daylily   daylily   daylily
    daylily   daylily   daylily   daylily   daylily
daylily   daylily   daylily   daylily   daylily   daylily
    daylily   daylily   daylily   daylily   daylily
daylily   daylily   daylily   daylily   daylily   daylily
    daylily   daylily   daylily   daylily   daylily
daylily   daylily   daylily   daylily   daylily   daylily
    daylily   daylily   daylily   daylily   daylily
daylily   daylily   daylily   daylily   daylily   daylily
    daylily   daylily   daylily   daylily   daylily
daylily   daylily   daylily   daylily   daylily   daylily
    daylily   daylily   daylily   daylily   daylily
daylily   daylily   daylily   daylily   daylily   daylily
    daylily   daylily   daylily   daylily   daylily
daylily   daylily   daylily   daylily   daylily   daylily

In a Heraclitean Sort of Way One Never Picks the Same Lily Twice

When I finish my task in this world
I shall gather the lilies

one by one

and set them before you—

        but not until then

Cut But Still Breathing

I watched the sky heap one cloud
                              on top of the other
The lilies dead
                  or cut but still breathing, stuffed

in boxes, printed papers, worn on fitted
shirts with arms and sleeves and a beautiful face
for carrying the bouquet up the aisle

Or was it *down* the aisle?

One never knows with lilies—
                              whether happiness or grief
marks the occasion
            or why they were cut in the first place

Lily Candescence

A lily by any other name
        would be a petal of the sun
                as the sun falls to earth

        When light from yonder window breaks
and sky disclaims excess,
           the lily, first thing in the morning,
        first light of day,
calls it not dawn but
           candescence

La Valse des Hémérocalles

This also is a story from long ago when the rivers carried
the goods of a nation from one century to the next and my
windows faced *la Butte-aux-Cailles* where the light would
go to experiment with the notion of sepia, a nostalgia that
I thought of as *la valse des hémérocalles*

That summer a long line of lilies not far from my rooms were
banked on the square spoken of as remembrance and memory,
a cloister of them, tall in their uniforms, elegant in that French
sort of way, a swagger in the small of the breeze
       as they re-arranged their collars,
               adjusted their sleeves

Mysteries of the Universe

I have a book of matches in my pocket
for no reason whatsoever but for something to read

I have three dimes and a quarter
that serve no purpose whatsoever but to add up

I have stardust from stones I collected along the shore
original quartz and granite from the solar system

I have a hole in my heart that my lover put there
so I would have something to say

I have the lines to a song I stuffed in a pocket
waiting for the phone to ring

I have a license, a passport, keys and nowhere to go
but out the front door

I have an electric razor in the bathroom which I never use
and lilies in the garden which I can't explain

Everlasting

No one really knows the true story of Li Bai and his secret lover
who went off together to gather the long-stem lilies they called
Forget-Sadness-Grass, the two of them on a walk in the woods,
myself not far behind and late July, the sun on a streak, the
planets lined up, the words between them filling the pages of
my book

Love is only as everlasting as an afternoon
Beauty of the kind that's true only ever as brief—
A lily laments the first light of the moon

So said Li Bai, his lover all ears

But when he spoke the wind was blowing across the tall grass
and the lilies changed his words forever

– II –
"Wild Thing"

Four Poems After E.D. Blodgett

— HANDS, THE DUST OF AGEING

The past behind me, writing in the summer heat,
the summer sun sculpted on the sky in sunset mode

Hard not to believe in elements of ice and silence,
rivers in their endings, autumn bound to come and bind me

to cycles of engagement
And there where summer marks

the dust of ageing, fingers intertwined,
expectations folded, hands clasped behind my back

— THE PATIENCE OF WATER

The patience of water lying flat on the pond
The fish that need know nothing to swim away
The moon a stone no bigger than the eye contains

The weather over my roof rests in my hands
The mountains on my cheeks
I represent an algorithm as consistently my own

I sound the soup of rain dimming as it falls to pieces
Birds that bend and swim the air each within its law
I take the shape of lilies to my bed

Exorbitant, the stars, the ones that stay
Long after I calculate the sum of all remaining days

MY CHEEKS ARE DRY AND CHILDLESS

I found the words "tears have lives/seeking mothers"
in a poem of his

I added tears of my own to the line and wrote
"they are the children for whom we have no words"

I spoke of flowers as only flowers speak of lasting long
(it was almost for an entire day)

I spoke of him in our mother tongue
and not a word between us when I laid him down to rest

WEEDS PERHAPS

What to bring your garden
now that your garden is dead and forgotten
under the autumn rain?

Lilies would be redundant
like roses when my father died in May,
their heads bowed and bent

If not lilies, then what?

For my father's wish to live out winter,
the roses buried with him,
I scattered vague, persistent seeds
on stone-cold ground,
weeds perhaps that might outlive us all

A Lily at the Window

There are half
degrees of light,
partial degrees
of heat, gradients
of thermonuclear
explosions
in the sphere
closest to home

Measured for lumens,
refraction,
thermal expansion,
the reach of its rays,
the age of the soul,
a lily returns
to the place
where you first saw it

—Coda

Three lilies with their face in the sun,
                their mouths wide open—

Not a word have they to say to me, yet
          can't stop talking when I'm not listening

Mirabilis

Grant you, I obsess over the slant of a roof,
            the angle of dormers,
      the washboard chatter of the wind

I insist on colours
                  I insist on numbers on a door
      I succumb to the beauty of pairs

There's a thrill to reading words
                  for the very first time

I marvel at grace, elegance,
                  the mention of being surprised,
meeting Glenn Gould on an afternoon
                  of my own invention

I marvel at the charm of the lilies

Who was it said,
To be astonished is one of the surest ways
            of not getting old too quickly?

I sit on a bench, my back dug into the slats,
                  and I wonder

Keeping a Low Profile

Pumped at the thought of ingenuity
as ingenuous—the rocket launch
of leaves into space, how trees learn
to behave themselves—and

wading through a pile of papers
just to get to where I am, well, there's
more than a day inside of one, and
more than one inside a year

Remarkable, the harmony of favours
I've received, so many came with wings
of admiration, trees growing taller
by the minute telling me I should stay put,

keep to myself and, like daylilies come July,
reappear just once a year

Eternity and *Lily*

Some words click like stones
I pick and pocket
or throw into the realm I deem
                    "out there"

and some words reach and some don't stick,
don't stick to a thing of what they mean
                    when I say them

Take two words, *Eternity* and *Lily*,
one heavy as a boulder,
a mountain's back,
the head on your shoulders,
no easy burden for Sisyphus to carry
to the summit of an incline plane—
heavy as what he can't forget

The other word—
light as a pebble, easy to hold,
                    easy to let go

Folk Song

Big ideas come down from the hills
　　　　get lost among the leaves
　　　　　　　once they spring to mind

Big trees get bigger every day
　　　　up to a certain point
　　　　just to say nothing lingers
　　　　　　　beyond its time

Same goes for the big ones of the valley
Day after day sucking at the tit of the IGA
Cheap bouquets by the check-out

Bye-bye lilies, it's the last I'll see of you today,
　　　　　gone to God knows where

The pretty pinks have also gone
　　　　and the banjo-picking peepers

One more plucked and strummed,
　　　　　　　one more lily
gone from the cool green hills of the valley

Drip Paintings

— —

Lily's
getting older,
obsessive, messy,
dripping with confessions, wet
with the fresh paint of sunsets

— —

in the poetry of living long
or dying young
what's a day when your life's
cut short
but still can fit a poem?

— —

Lily's cane supports a dying wish—
face it (her words not mine)
no one needs a second set of knees

we fall on one, leave on the other

—~

we're all painted,
children alike,
to stand on our own two feet

in her use of shadows
Lily records an end to summer

Lily buys herself some time

—~

it's true we all begin
to look like dead leaves
(lilies, sunsets, Labour Day)
when the paint goes dry

Daily

a lily is
      a lily is
            a lily is
                 a lily is

how I keep track of time

I ask nothing of my work but that it returns to me

daylily
      daylily
            daylily
                 daylily
                       daylily
                             daylily

Chasing the Fact

In a forest of tall slender maples,
                              craters the size of a moon
I felt no bigger than a snail in a wilderness of lilies
The sap was cooling and moving slowly,
                              curling like a tail of smoke
No faster
I ran a red light in a world completely devoid of red lights
No one knew
I had reason to believe in the impossible
My chassis as I found out
                    was branded with a Fibonacci sequence
As if I needed an explanation
As if a little engine ran my heart
And families bloomed on the horizon

Creation

A cloud is where you see it and it isn't where you don't.
—John Ruskin

There are jays and squirrels, red ones and grays,
Downy and hairy woodpeckers, juncos, two kinds
          of nuthatches
                    and chickadees in the trees

There should be a muskrat and a raven
Clouds where I put them
Lilies where the pond is a clear-top table of glass

There's even a red wheelbarrow
                    and four white chickens
                              named Paulette

There are advantages to being wild in
                    a jungle of tall grasses

And by the woodshed there have always been
          degrees of happiness
                    and lookouts and interludes

I provide the feeders for a spectacle, birds and
                              seeds for the masses

I provide the aftermath for putting ideas in your head
          reflections in the pond
                    that have nothing to do with me
                    or lying down in a sentence

The Light at the Foot of Round Top

Birds don't know the words to the songs they sing

The wind can't read the pages of the book
                                    in my hands

Words of the heavenly dad, mother of us all,
                    don't seem right at this latitude
where the sky is a cold accomplice, Round Top rising
and holding back the sun

It's morning everywhere around the world
            at least once a day (I know that for a fact)
and who couldn't use a hand getting up out of bed

These orange daylilies I've been telling you about
                    know all about the workings of the sun
Watch them take all the light for themselves

Their eyes in the pond perplex the dawn,
                                    myself as well—
            gone the moment I look

"Wild Thing"

Rain-reflected light
        dazzling on beads of dew
                dripped on the iris of the lilies,
eyes that glorify the sun,
       the clouds off and on as distant gray matter
that's no match
            for what goes on inside our heads

Flowers driven by the speed
                  and volume of the rising sun,
an accordion of light breathing in and out of shadows
        with a sigh

        I'm 41 (maybe I'm 71)
    and I've never heard a peep from the sun

Pretty birds,
           the yellow finch, like sun drops
on a pine bough

How lonely I'd be
      if it weren't for the songs I have them sing,
                the wings I wear

Again, this morning, the sun jumped up into the sky
              and where it fell
                the light was suffused
with the glowing knowledge
              it had been there before

"Wild Thing" is what I heard, and in my head,
        that's the song
                the birds were singing

Green Space

I have always admired the deep shadows
                                  in the forest,
the dark blots where the deer
                        conceal themselves
and out of which they bravely step into the world

I am convinced I don't belong here,
                  and if I do I must be still, hold
my breath and count my blessings,
                  get metaphysical with time and space
where the mystery of this woodlot meets
                            the 21st century

I'm not that far from eternity, not at my age—
              the hollyhock says so, and the lily
                   and black-eyed Susan

End of summer says so too,
                    close to the end of its tether

Tall trees dominate the skyline—tall trees connected
             to the starlight that I can't see from here
at the edge of all that's green in space

The Last of Them

Early morning begins a poem that puts the sun right,
pulls it out from underneath the trees
                          and looks it in the eye

A poem can stare at the sun for the longest time,
          can drown in the palm
of your hand, the pond, the lake, and still come up for air

Dawn of first light at the water's edge
                          writing lines the waves recite

Pleated clouds, one after another, like tissues
out of a Kleenex box, scudding, colliding
          one into the other inside a poet's head
where the evergreens reside upside down
                    and the last of the lilies float
                          towards the edge of the page

Lyric with a Line by Charles Wright

I found *the lethargy of a single cloud*
                              in a poem by Wright

where the poet turns his eyes
                    towards the sky
            and a solitary cloud is passing by

            not bothered in the least knowing
that it's never the same cloud twice
                    on a second glance

Forget Sadness

I'm reminded what Camus said,
                         that we spend our life
looking for the way back
to the few simple truths we knew from the start

Mom's wooden spoon
                  Dad's fishing lures
                              The friends I lost in transit
My street address when I was born
                                  That God is good
                  but too far to bother with
The truth of pi and two-wheel bikes
The best places to hide
                  The power of positive thinking
Halloween

                              There's more to be said
but for now the shelves are barren
         and the lilies are beginning to die off—
were never meant to last this long
                  or face the waste of winter

I know the world will seem empty without them,
         I'll miss their eyes in the pond's reflections
and I won't know where to look anymore,
         the two chairs on the other side empty, one
                  of them always empty

The sun's slowing down and has fallen behind,
                  setting where it's never set before
A short time from now the light will go missing
and the last of the lilies will leave the tall grasses

Forget sadness—it's in their name—
         soon we'll all be gone, and gone for good

One Last Look

Late light once again, but light rising
                  from a different poem

one that's about
         to begin
      on the same side of the page
              and come to an end
                  on the other

The sun packs a wallop
      all day up on its toes
              and my missing the lilies

my missing the tall forget-all-that-sadness-stuff
      abounding at the pond
all day back in the city
        waiting to see
           what happens next

And everything that happened
      up until now had happened next

The market came and went
The bakery closed at five
Amazon delivered the goods

In the present it is all done
as it was once done before—
                              easing into happiness
pine steeples taller
                  flight plans to nowhere fixed
oak leaves turning colour
            mums in respite
pools of gravel grey
              reflections evaporating
                        into early autumn
                                    and on my sleeves
a circumstance of rooftops, windows, eaves
and clouds that rub their eyes for one last look

Stage Lily

The instruction manual says it's the end of the day
There's nothing more to be done without the sun

But here comes the wood thrush
                                    and his sky-high whistling
sliding scales among leaves so familiar
                        I know them by heart,
crows in the distance on baritone and bass

                    And I'm thinking, why call it a day—
I can still see the lily perked up on the stage,
        bliss on her cheeks, the blush of possibility
spread all over her face,
                            a song in her throat
                        darkness avoiding the white of her eyes

Follow the Deer

Mother shines her boots the old-fashioned way

She brings out the gloss
       of years that have gone from her face

The deer live for the sole purpose
           of finding her footprints,
              nibbling at the leaves
she leaves behind

She is all for symbiosis and David Suzuki

She is all for the rain that must fall

The deer too, Mother says, shall rest at her feet

But deer are without wings and they must circle
                  and circle
before they sleep,
        their dreams stuffed inside clouds
that hide the moon,
       their faces in the tremble of the night

And come day, I, too, see myself
         in the polish of Mother's boots
and I follow her footsteps

                I follow the deer

Witness Statement

Here in the mountains
that cross the border
between us and them
anything unusual goes
unreported, we mind
our own bees' wax, and
nothing goes missing
or is lost for long—it all
turns up in the snowmelt
or hanging, silver and bright,
from the beak of a crow

Who can you trust?
The calendar says one thing,
the leaves preach something else

If I turn my gaze to the back
of my head and dwell on what's
gone past
everything changes
and the mountains are gone

If I look ahead,
nothing but valleys
and peaks
I keep to myself

October Issue

It appears in boxes

Predictions of poppies to come, *Popular Mechanics,*
    People Magazine, The Walrus, Poetry,
        mums in multiplex semi-autumn tones,
the latter half of October like a lonely part-time
        drop-out on a campus call to mom

I'm here, am I not?

        Decades later it's still October, a bag
    of bones and second-rate lifetimes in rehearsal
searching for a simile to suggest a resurrection back
        to younger days

    When the mums were fire red,
        and the lilies not all dead

Catherine Deneuve's Heartbeat

I'm listening to Catherine Deneuve's heartbeat in bed while
Caroline Shaw's *Some Bright Morning*, a concerto for wings
and voices performed by the songbirds of Sō Percussion,
accompanies a memory I've dusted off with a chance
encounter of *madeleines* that take me home to a time of
quilted petals, soft as feathers, where lilies at the window
were the only blossoms and my pillow

Socrates,

once consumed
by navel gazing
with a little imagination
refined the selfie
to get beneath
the skin

if that's rain
he hears
he'll expect to get wet
if he doesn't
like what he sees
he'll change the image

(my daughter
if I had one
would say the same)

thunder rumbles
because
that's the word
we have for it

birds
because they're
everywhere

lilies
where they stand
stand
to face the sun

if the belly's knot
is the first
and final
point of contact
with the known

then the unreflected
selfie's not
worth taking

From the Top of Round Top

Suddenly you land
on your feet
and you're on
your toes
peering over a ledge
(in this case the top
of the page)
which resembles
the lip of all
the literal chasms
you've ever been up against,
peak after peak,
and an even longer descent
to the bottom
of the page
where the lilies
are resting

Target Practice

Harmonies
in second
person plurals
written
like tall grasses
waving
in the distance,
a function of
the image
on the page
if that is all
we have to say

Conflicts
written
in first
person singular
with words
like missiles
pounding
in the distance,
a function of
my finger
on the trigger
if that was all
I had to say

Crushed Spiders

There are consequences—
My foolish Valentine
My drafty quarters
My metaphors on display
                        for display purposes only

Sweet memories go round
And round inside my head
Pretty soon I'll want
The real thing instead
                        So I sing these words

I'm not lonely, I'm just lingering
Gas tanks explode
People get killed
Things are meant to be for real

Like kisses and mistletoe
The roses about to die
The web of lies above my pillow
The bed of lilies on my side

Virgil by the Fountain

After 2000 years Virgil is still writing, more or less,
                         about the very same things

There are no lilies in heaven, he reminds us,
                         only here on earth

And the garden bench is a necessary extrapolation
                         of the original bench
where he sits and sees himself
          afloat with the lilies stirred in the fountain

Light begins when you first open your eyes,
                         ends when you close them

Nothing's changed there

Poets are known to put things like that into words
                         It's what they do

It's all they do
          like Virgil did, year after year in the lap
                         of the fountain

Overlooking the Skating Pond,
the Lilies Go Missing

—after John Ashbery

A beautiful occasion on a Saturday night
unwrapped in a ring, strings of memory ravelling
around the square, snapping fingers in pharmaceutical
happiness, metaphors like a unison out of season

I can't see any further from my chair, passing lights, big
bird chimes, the wind shivering
through the low-lying ivy boughs, a concussion of tropes
usually found in broken lines

Opinions on holiday-making and the extreme right
are worth the extra weight and waiver, how sweat
gets stored away, it's almost seven, the bells
can't help themselves, once around the frozen pond

the skaters go both fast and slow
not so much because I remember where I am but I put myself
in the picture, paint myself into a corner, create
impressions good enough to pass as real

But some come loose, slither into bushes

The ice melting

Fountains back in order

A village green, fat with points of view

Le Regard

Like a Roman statue, I watch everything and see nothing.
— Charles Wright

Music stirs the air,
                    earbuds tucked in place,
a ripple at the water's edge breaking
        where the lilies make a living
                                with a heart
and no place to go

                    Late afternoon, granite sky,
there is no time like the present
        to see the tall trees lean
in the direction they will fall one day

At the fountain's edge, the waters stunned
                        by the first shock of ice,
the ducks and geese calling out warnings:
                    there could be a storm in our future

There is a strong probability
                    that we all see what we want to see,
that perplexity is in the eye of the beholder
            and pure simplicity in the thing itself

                        I've looked both ways
when it comes to crossing the road,
            all my life actually,
and the other side is always straight ahead

Human Emotions

Bees are enriched
        geranium reactors, serious business
radiating antonyms for total annihilation

It takes one to know one
        is the buzz in the bee world
Bees need to keep busy

To feed themselves they proceed
        according to rank: they have their place
in the great grand scheme of things

The hive is bigger than a human brain
        It can stretch and pull in all directions
Even to the ends of the earth

Dendrites, six-sided polygons, apertures,
        rhizomes, petals, plasticity
are often on our minds, and always present

among the bees
        Like it is with you and me,
tranquility resembles the hum that generates

a grounded state of being
        of which the end product, as usual,
is sticky and sweet

The Scarf

The gulls come from nothing, right out of thin air
The idea that we all have to come from somewhere
                            is in the crook of their wings,
the crest they drag behind them

See how the lake folds and takes hold of their descent
                      to measure the distance they cover

Their bodies defy gravity and plunge

How they call to me says who they are

Surfers, seagulls, vultures, geese, swans soft
                              in the arms of the bay
                  proliferate every place I look

Wings depend on water, the widening of waves,
                    waves that bring a field of emotions
reproduced in the arc of a wing,
the air fat with distance
                    and not a word to be heard

The moon is a fossil
The oak tree an eminence
The lily rising from the grave says
                        we all love to grow

A woman of no known provenance
     does a dance with the waves
where the water's edge laps at her feet

A thought bubble floats in the air above her
I put it there, close to where
  the water's silk along the shore is wet

Will she fly away and, just like that, disappear
    back into nothing, back to nowhere?
Or like the gulls this morning and the swans,
   leave her scarf adrift in the hands of the wind?

The Landing

The swans keep coming back and
          make me think of her
               now that she is gone

I often think of Susan dead
          and run the risk of sentimentality,
of finding purpose in a metaphor,
       landing where the ducks also come to land
               and don't sink

That Song

May as well talk to the lilies
                 than question myself, ask if they
                        remember The Doors,
that song about the end and Jim Morrison
                    so close to the answer himself

But I prefer the silence that comes in their response,
                    how it detonates the wind
as petals fall and heartbreaks are further broken down
                       into cause and effect

Last night, meteors rained across the darkened heavens
                     and I didn't see a thing

Too early, I was told, or not late enough

I looked for as long as I could stand it and saw nothing
                 but the moon, a crescent,
                      and a million stars
that didn't seem to belong to the night

Of course, by then the daylilies
                 had already turned their faces away,
                    away from the inevitable
oblivion that comes at the end of that song

A Lyric Written in the Manner of Virgil

Birdsong through a panel of sunlight
The gold of light on green
And a breeze—a breeze about the size of a pea
And the feeder fixed on finches and birds of paradise
That I fill in from memory

It's all true
The sunlight and birdsong, the last of an afternoon
The trees and tall tufts of forget-sadness-grass
And the orange blaze of summer blooms
The gold and godlike gloaming of an afterthought

Imagine

that the sun has yet to leave
      and it's almost at the point of no return,
the time of day when the lustre dims
and lilies are bound to fall apart,
           cast off the shrapnel
        of petals in a soft explosion
that's made to be like that

the old ways of doubling up in the pond
                       are vanishing now,
the water's surface a blank page
           that keeps me guessing
what's real and what was once in deep reflection

trees are losing their sight
      and the big green spaces diminished,
flattened in the persistent gloaming,
                green to dark green
then black as blacktop on a clear-cut strip
        of disappearing highway

     then there's nothing to see
but darkness in near confrontation, the lilies
           clenched into a fist

Closing Time

Fool's gold
                    purple light
                            the dusk of time,
            the lily's final thrust
                    down to only minutes left

The overhanging maples lean,
                    tall pines net the last of light

Temples made of longing, branches

Fat moon riding bareback
                    up from the eastern coast

About These Poems

December is far from July, the daylilies long gone by then, the gardens a cold and stiffened brick of earth and fallen leaves, winter as literal as that, unlike the heat of summer when I sit by the tall Forget-Sadness-Grass bathing in light and with them thrive on the longest days, blossoms bursting out in pale, forgiving shades of tawny orange like no other colour in the universe.

I talk to them, read to them, send virtual letters to friends about them.

I say they live for only a day, celestial beings, open-faced from dawn till the last of light.

I say "muse" and they nod their heads in my direction.

Not a true *Lilium*, nonetheless they are the most delicate of blossoms, elegant and lithe, tall, winsome, sturdy. We sometimes call them *Hemerocallis Fulva* of the constellation *Asphodelaceae*, or they are mistakenly referred to as tiger lilies. The daylily, as you can see, has many names and appears in a host of different manifestations.

December is far from July and all that lingers of the lily come winter are these poems, each one drawn from the gardens by the pond and the roads that lead away from where we live, the lilies dead by the end of the day, brief as a poem when you turn the page or close the book.

And as sure as July follows December, the lilies return and the poems remain.

NOTES & ACKNOWLEDGEMENTS

Some of these poems have appeared in the following journals, chapbooks, and anthologies, sometimes with a different title and/or in a different form: *Devour; Event; Exile, Poetry Present; Subterranean Blue Poetry; Lessons from the Earth* (eChapbook 2020, ed. Jessica Outram); *Spirit of the Hills Arts Anthology* (2020, ed. Susan Stratham); *Our Pandemic Times* (Blue Denim Press, 2021, ed. Felicity Sidnell Reid and Kim Aubrey); *True Identity* (Hidden Brook Press, 2021, ed. April Blumer); *Voices of Quebec* (League of Canadian Poets Chapbook, 2021, ed. Carolyne Van Der Meer).

The Chinese ideogram for *Hemerocallis Fulva*, 百合, literally means Forget-Sadness-Grass.

In "Journal Entry," the lines by Tseng Jui (ca. 1300) are from his poem, "Sheep on Mountain Slope" in *Sunflower Splendor* (Princeton University Press, 1975, ed. Wu-Chi Liu and Irving Lo).

In "Thousands of Lilies," the epigraph is by Li Bai (ca. 750) in "Song of Hsiang-yang" also found in *Sunflower Splendor.*

"Four Poems After E.D. Blodgett" recognizes the sweeping lyricism of his award-winning book, *Apostrophe: Woman at the Piano* (Buschek-Books, 1996). The titles are taken from his poems.

In "*Mirabilis*," the line "To be astonished . . ." is by Colette and was found etched into a park bench in the gardens of le Palais Royal in Paris.

In "Lyric with a Line by Charles Wright," the line comes from his book, *Sestet* (Farrar Straus & Giroux, 2009).

"Catherine Deneuve's Heartbeat" references Caroline Shaw's song, "Some Bright Morning," from the album, *Let the Soil Play Its Simple Part*, performed by Sō Percussion (Nonesuch, June 2020). To paraphrase her words, *a lily is a lily is a lily is a lily is how I keep track of time.*

I found a wealth of poetry in the anthology, *Sunflower Splendor: Three Thousand Years of Chinese Poetry* (Princeton University Press, 1975, ed. by Wu-Chi Liu and Irving Lo). Li Bai is another name for the poet I first knew as Li Po who lived and wrote during the T'ang Dynasty.

I am grateful to Kate Rogers, my editor on this book, whose keen eye and ear and insights into the Chinese language gave these poems the attention to detail they deserved. Her comments and suggestions were not only welcomed but, like a gentle summer rain, refreshing.

And I am grateful to the following friends and colleagues who have been personal champions of poetry in all its forms: Richard (Tai) and Kim Grove, Laurence Hutchman, Carolyne Van Der Meer, Felicity Sidnell Reid, Gwen Sheltema, Kim Aubrey, John B. Lee, Miguel Olivé Iglesias of the University of Holguin in Cuba, Jorge Alberto Hernandez, Rania Jaber, Jessica Outram, Wally Keeler, Ted Amsden, James Pickersgill and the members of the Cobourg Poetry Workshop, my publishers in Vancouver, Kevin Welsh and Wendy Atkinson, and especially to Annie, whose gardens are the reason these poems exist.

Finally, I wish to offer the gift of a lily to the memory of Ronald Hatch, founder of Ronsdale Press and a true champion of the written word.

ABOUT THE AUTHOR

 Antony Di Nardo is a full-time poet and editor. He was born in Montreal and obtained a post-graduate degree in English from the University of Toronto. His writing career began as a journalist, publishing and editing a weekly newspaper in northwestern Ontario, and contributing poetry to the first issues of *The Squatchberry Journal.* He is the author of seven books of poetry, his most recent, *Through Yonder Window Breaks,* having won the inaugural Don Gutteridge Poetry Prize. His work has been translated into several languages and appears widely in journals and anthologies. He divides his time between Sutton, Quebec and Cobourg, Ontario.